Go
Van
Go!

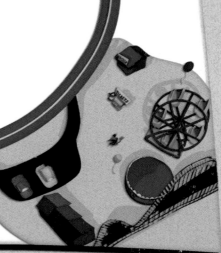

One night the Flugelhorn family decided to take a road trip.

    Noah wanted to go to the cottage.

    Anna wanted to go to the fair.

    Dad wanted to go to the beach.

    Mom wanted to go camping.

    Randolph just wanted his bone.

They went to bed singing their special road-trip song:

Zzuh zzuh vroom vroom go Van Go!
Where we're going we don't know.
Heading down the interstate,
Hurry Mom or we'll be late.
Zzuh zzuh vroom vroom go Van Go!

The next morning, the Flugelhorn family went to the cottage.

Noah packed Fluffbottom the super bunny.

Anna packed her CD player.

Dad packed his fishing pole.

Mom packed raincoats.

And Randolph packed a bone.

They drove off singing:

Zzuh zzuh vroom vroom go Van Go!
Where we're going we don't know.
Heading down the interstate,
Hurry Mom or we'll be late.
Zzuh zzuh vroom vroom go Van Go!

But then Mom said, "Did I remember the soap?"

The next morning, the family went to the fair.
Noah packed Mr. Growls the polar bear.
Anna packed her sunglasses.
Dad packed his appetite.
Mom packed walkie-talkies.
And Randolph packed a bone.

VAN GO

17 JZ

EXIT

They drove off singing:

Zzuh zzuh vroom vroom go Van Go!
Where we're going we don't know.
Heading down the interstate,
Hurry Mom or we'll be late.
Zzuh zzuh vroom vroom go Van Go!

But then Dad said, "Has anyone seen my fishing pole?"

The next morning the family went to the beach.
Noah packed Creepy the crocodile.
Anna packed her polka-dot towel.
Dad packed his book.
Mom packed the sunscreen.
And Randolph packed a bone.

They drove off singing:

Zzuh zzuh vroom vroom go Van Go!
Where we're going we don't know.
Heading down the interstate,
Hurry Mom or we'll be late.
Zzuh zzuh vroom vroom go Van Go!

But then Anna said, "Have you seen my sunglasses?"

The next morning the family went camping.
Noah packed Hopalong the kangaroo.
Anna packed her lip gloss.
Dad packed his binoculars.
Mom packed bug spray.
And Randolph packed a bone.

They drove off singing:

Zzuh zzuh vroom vroom go Van Go!
Where we're going we don't know.
Heading down the interstate,
Hurry Mom or we'll be late.
Zzuh zzuh vroom vroom go Van Go!

But then Noah said, "Where's Creepy?"

That afternoon the family went hiking,
and the forest animals came out to play.

The next morning the family went home.
Noah packed his backpack.
Anna packed her duffle.
Dad packed the cooler.
Mom packed the first-aid kit.
And Randolph packed a bone.

They drove off singing:

Zzuh zzuh vroom vroom go Van Go!
Where we're going we don't know.
Heading down the interstate,
Hurry Mom or we'll be late.
Zzuh zzuh vroom vroom go Van Go!

But then they all said, "Where's Randolph?"

The next day the family unpacked Van Go.
Noah found Creepy.
Anna found her sunglasses.
Dad found his fishing pole.
Mom found the soap.
And Randolph found all his bones.

They went to bed singing:
Zzuh zzuh vroom vroom go Van Go!
Where we're going we don't know.
Heading down the interstate,
Hurry Mom or we'll be late.
Zzuh zzuh vroom vroom go Van Go!

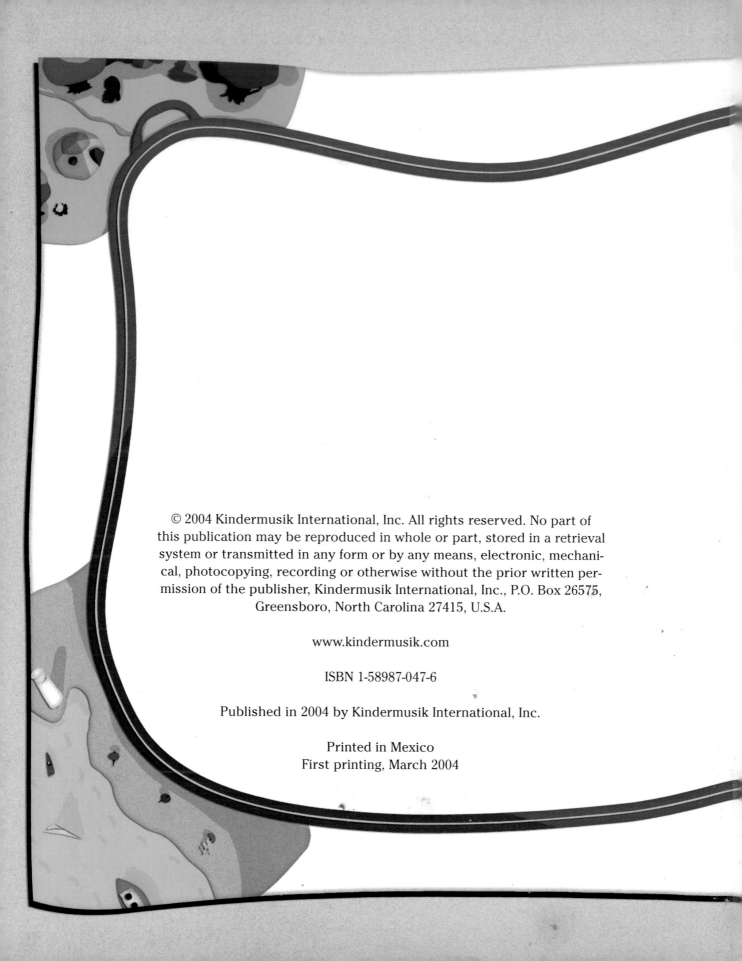

www.kindermusik.com

ISBN 1-58987-047-6

Published in 2004 by Kindermusik International, Inc.

Printed in Mexico
First printing, March 2004